BEECHENBROOK

MORE WILDSIDE CLASSICS

BEECHENBROOK

A RHYME OF THE WAR

MARGARET J. PRESTON

WILDSIDE PRESS

BEECHENBROOK

This edition published 2005 by Wildside Press, LLC.
www.wildsidepress.com

CONTENTS

BEECHENBROOK

I.

There is sorrow in Beechenbrook Cottage; the day
Has been bright with the earliest glory of May;
The blue of the sky is as tender a blue
As ever the sunshine came shimmering through:
The songs of the birds and the hum of the bees,
As they merrily dart in and out of the trees,—
The blooms of the orchard, as sifting its snows,
It mingles its odors with hawthorn and rose,—
The voice of the brook, as it lapses unseen,—
The laughter of children at play on the green,—
Insist on a picture so cheerful, so fair,
Who ever would dream that a grief could be there!

The last yellow sunbeam slides down from the wall,
The purple of evening is ready to fall;
The gladness of daylight is gone, and the gloom
Of something like sadness is over the room.
Right bravely all day, with a smile on her brow,
Has Alice been true to her duty,—but now
Her tasks are all ended,—naught inside or out,
For the thoughtfullest love to be busy about;
The knapsack well furnished, the canteen all bright,
The soldier's grey dress and his gauntlets in sight,
The blanket tight strapped, and the haversack stored,
And lying beside them, the cap and the sword;
No last, little office,—no further commands,—
No service to steady the tremulous hands;
All wife-work,—the sweet work that busied her so,
Is finished:—the dear one is ready to go.

Not a sob has escaped her all day,–not a moan;
But now the tide rushes,–for she is alone.
On the fresh, shining knapsack she pillows her head,
And weeps as a mourner might weep for the dead.
She heeds not the three-year old baby at play,
As donning the cap, on the carpet he lay;
Till she feels on her forehead, his fingers' soft tips,
And on her shut eyelids, the touch of his lips.

"Mamma is *so* sorry!–Mamma is *so* sad!
But Archie can make her look up and be glad:
I've been praying to God, as you told me to do,
That Papa may come back when the battle is thro':–
He says when we pray, that our prayers shall be heard;
And Mamma, don't you *always* know, God keeps his word?"

Around the young comforter stealthily press
The arms of his father with sudden caress;
Then fast to his heart,–love and duty at strife,–
He snatches with fondest emotion, his wife.

"My own love! my precious!–I feel I am strong;
I know I am brave in opposing the wrong;
I could stand where the battle was fiercest, nor feel
One quiver of nerve at the flash of the steel;
I could gaze on the enemy guiltless of fears,
But I quail at the sight of your passionate tears:
My calmness forsakes me,–my thoughts are a-whirl,
And the stout-hearted man is as weak as a girl.

I've been proud of your fortitude; never a trace
Of yielding, all day, could I read in your face;
But a look that was resolute, dauntless and high,
As ever flashed forth from a patriot's eye.
I know how you cling to me,—know that to part
Is tearing the tenderest cords of your heart:
Through the length and the breadth of our Valley to-day,
No hand will a costlier sacrifice lay
On the altar of Country; and Alice,—sweet wife!
I never have worshipped you so in my life!
Poor heart,—that has held up so brave in the past,—
Poor heart! must it break with its burden at last?"

The arms thrown about him, but tighten their hold,
The cheek that he kisses, is ashy and cold,
And bowed with the grief she so long has suppressed,
She weeps herself quiet and calm on his breast.
At length, in a voice just as steady and clear
As if it had never been choked by a tear,
She raises her eyes with a softened control,
And through them her husband looks into her soul.

"I feel that we each for the other could die;
Your heart to my own makes the instant reply:
But dear as you are, Love,—my life and my light,—
I would not consent to your stay, if I might:
No!—arm for the conflict, and on, with the rest;
Virginia has need of her bravest and best!
My heart—it must bleed, and my cheek will be wet,
Yet never, believe me, with selfish regret:
My ardor abates not one jot of its glow,
Though the tears of the wife and the woman *will* flow.

"Our cause is so holy, so just, and so true,—
Thank God! I can give a defender like you!
For home, and for children,—for freedoms—for bread,—
For the house of our God,—for the graves of our dead,—
For leave to exist on the soil of our birth,—
For everything manhood holds dearest on earth:
When *these* are the things that we fight for—dare I
Hold back my best treasure, with plaint or with sigh?
My cheek would blush crimson,—my spirit be galled,
If *he* were not there when the muster was called!
When we pleaded for peace, every right was denied;
Every pressing petition turned proudly aside;
Now God judge betwixt us!—God prosper the right!
To brave men there's nothing remains, but to fight:
I grudge you not, Douglass,—die, rather than yield,—
And like the old heroes,—come home on your shield!"

The morning is breaking:—the flush of the dawn
Is warning the soldier, 'tis time to be gone;
The children around him expectantly wait,—
His horse, all caparisoned, paws at the gate:
With face strangely pallid,—no sobbings,—no sighs,—
But only a luminous mist in her eyes,
His wife is subduing the heart-throbs that swell,
And calming herself for a quiet farewell.

There falls a felt silence:—the note of a bird,
A tremulous twitter,—is all that is heard;
The circle has knelt by the holly-bush there,—
And listen,—there comes the low breathing of prayer.

"Father! fold thine arms of pity
    Round us as we lowly bow;
Never have we kneeled before Thee
    With such burden'd hearts as now!

Joy has been our constant portion,
    And if ill must now befall,
With a filial acquiescence,
    We would thank thee for it all.

In the path of present duty,
    With Thy hand to lean upon,
Questioning not the hidden future,
    May we walk serenely on.

For this holy, happy home-love,
    Purest bliss that crowns my life,—
For these tender, trusting children,—
    For this fondest, faithful wife,—

Here I pour my full thanksgiving;
    And, when heart is torn from heart,
Be our sweetest tryst-word, '*Mizpah*,'—
    Watch betwixt us while we part!

And if never round this altar,
    We should kneel as heretofore,—
If these arms in benediction
    Fold my precious ones no more,—

Thou, who in her direst anguish,
    Sooth'dst thy mother's lonely lot,
In thy still unchanged compassion,
    Son of Man! forsake them not!"

The little ones each he has caught to his breast,
And clasped them, and kissed them with fervent caress;
Then wordless and tearless, with hearts running o'er,
They part who have never been parted before:
He springs to his saddle,—the rein is drawn tight,—
And Beechenbrook Cottage is lost to his sight.

II.

The feathery foliage has broadened its leaves,
And June, with its beautiful mornings and eves,
Its magical atmosphere, breezes and blooms,
Its woods all delicious with thousand perfumes,—
First-born of the Summer,—spoiled pet of the year,—
June, delicate queen of the seasons, is here!

The sadness has passed from the dwelling away,
And quiet serenity brightens the day:
With innocent prattle, her toils to beguile,
In the midst of her children, the mother *must* smile.
With matronly cares,—those relentless demands
On the strength of her heart and the skill of her hands,—
The hours come tenderly, ceaselessly fraught,
And leave her small space for the broodings of thought.

Thank God!—busy fingers a solace can find,
To lighten the burden of body or mind;
And Eden's old curse proves a blessing instead,—
"In the sweat of thy brow shalt thou toil for thy bread."
For the bless'd relief in all labours that lurk,
Aye, thank Him, unhappy ones,—thank Him for work!

Thus Alice engages her thoughts and her powers,
And industry kindly lends wings to the hours:
Poor, petty employments they sometimes appear,
And on her bright needle there plashes a tear,—
Half shame and half passion;—what would she not dare
Her fervid compatriots' struggles to share?
It irks her,—the weakness of womanhood then,—
Yet such are the tears that make heroes of men!

She feels the hot blood of the nation beat high;
With rapture she catches the rallying cry:
From mountain and valley and hamlet they come!
On every side echoes the roll of the drum.
A people as firm, as united, as bold,
As ever drew blade for the blessings they hold,
Step sternly and solemnly forth in their might,
And swear on their altars to die for the right!

The clangor of muskets,—the flashing of steel,—
The clatter of spurs on the stout-booted heel,—
The waving of banners,—the resonant tramp
Of marching battalions,—the fiery stamp
Of steeds in their war-harness, newly decked out,—
The blast of the bugle,—the hurry, the shout,—
The terrible energy, eager and wild,
That lights up the face of man, woman and child,—
That burns on all lips, that arouses all powers;
Did ever we dream that such times would be ours?

One thought is absorbing, with giant control,—
With deadliest earnest, the national soul:—
"The right of self-government, crown of our pride,—
Right, bought with the sacredest blood,—is denied!
Shall we tamely resign what our enemy craves?
No! martyrs we *may* be!—we *cannot* be slaves!"

Fair women who naught but indulgence have seen,
Who never have learned what denial could mean,—

Who deign not to clipper their own dainty feet,
Whose wants swarthy handmaids stand ready to meet,
Whose fingers decline the light kerchief to hem,—
What aid in this struggle is hoped for from them?

Yet see! how they haste from their bowers of ease,
Their dormant capacities fired,—to seize
Every feminine weapon their skill can command,—
To labor with head, and with heart, and with hand.
They stitch the rough jacket, they shape the coarse shirt,
Unheeding though delicate fingers be hurt;
They bind the strong haversack, knit the grey glove,
Nor falter nor pause in their service of love.

When ever were people subdued, overthrown,
With women to cheer them on, brave as our own?
With maidens and mothers at work on their knees,
When ever were soldiers as fearless as these?

June's flower-wreathed sceptre is dropped with a sigh,
And forth like an empress steps stately July:
She sits all unveiled, amidst sunshine and balms,
As Zenobia sat in her City of Palms!

Not yet has the martial horizon grown dun,
Not yet has the terrible conflict begun:
But the tumult of legions,—the rush and the roar,
Break over our borders, like waves on the shore.
Along the Potomac, the confident foe
Stands marshalled for onset,—prepared, at a blow,
To vanquish the daring rebellion, and fling
Utter ruin at once on the arrogant thing!

How sovran the silence that broods o'er the sky,
And ushers the twenty-first morn of July;
—Date, written in fire on history's scroll,—
—Date, drawn in deep blood-lines on many a soul!

There is quiet at Beechenbrook: Alice's brow
Is wearing a Sabbath tranquility now,
As softly she reads from the page on her knee,—
"Thou wilt keep him in peace who is stayed upon Thee!"
When Sophy bursts breathlessly into the room,—
"Oh! mother! we hear it,—we hear it!.., the boom
Of the fast and the fierce cannonading!—it shook
The ground till it trembled, along by the brook."

One instant the listener sways in her seat,—
The paralysed heart has forgotten to beat;
The next, with the speed and the frenzy of fear,
She gains the green hillock, and pauses to hear.

Again and again the reverberant sound
Is fearfully felt in the tremulous ground;
Again and again on their senses it thrills,
Like thunderous echoes astray in the hills.

On tip-toe,—the summer wind lifting his hair,
With nostril expanded, and scenting the air
Like a mettled young war-horse that tosses his mane,
And frettingly champs at the bit and the rein,—
Stands eager, exultant, a twelve-year-old boy,
His face all aflame with a rapturous joy.

"*That's* music for heroes in battle array!
Oh, mother! I feel like a Roman to-day!
The Romans I read of in Plutarch;—Yes, men
Thought it noble to die for their liberties then!
And I've wondered if soldiers were ever so bold,
So gallant and brave, as those heroes of old.
—There!—listen!—that volley peals out the reply;
They prove it is sweet for their country to die:
How grand it must be! what a pride! what a joy!
—And *I* can do nothing: I'm only a boy!"

The fervid hand drops as he ceases to speak,
And the eloquent crimson fades out on his cheek.

"Oh, Beverly!—brother! It never would do!
Who comforts mamma, and who helps her like you?
She sends to the battle her darlingest one,—
She could not give both of them,—husband and son;
If she lose *you*, what's left her in life to enjoy?
—Oh, no! I am *glad* you are only a boy."
And Sophy looks up with her tenderest air,
And kisses the fingers that toy with her hair.

For her, who all silent and motionless stands,
And over her heart locks her quivering hands,
With white lips apart, and with eyes that dilate,
As if the low thunder were sounding her fate,—
What racking suspenses, what agonies stir,
What spectres these echoes are rousing for her!

Brave-natur'd, yet quaking,—high-souled, yet so pale,—
Is it thus that the wife of a soldier should quail,
And shudder and shrink at the boom of a gun,
As only a faint-hearted girl should have done?
Ah! wait until custom has blunted the keen,
Cutting edge of that sound, and no woman, I ween,
Will hear it with pulses more equal, more free
From feminine terrors and weakness, than she.

The sun sinks serenely; a lingering look
He flings at the mists that steal over the brook,
Like nuns that come forth in the twilight to pray,
Till their blushes are seen through their mantles of grey.

The gay-hearted children, but lightly oppressed,
Find perfect relief on their pillow of rest:
For Alice, no bless'd forgetfulness comes;—
The wail of the bugles,—the roll of the drums,—
The musket's sharp crack,—the artillery's roar,—
The flashing of bayonets dripping with gore,—
The moans of the dying,—the horror, the dread,
The ghastliness gathering over the dead,—
Oh! these are the visions of anguish and pain,—
The phantoms of terror that troop through her brain!

She pauses again and again on the floor,
Which the moonlight has brightened so mockingly o'er;
She wrings her cold hands with a groan of despair;
—"Oh, God! have compassion!—my darling is there!"

All placidly, dewily, freshly, the dawn
Comes stealing in pulseless tranquility on:
More freely she breathes, in its balminess, though
The forehead it kisses is pallid with woe.

Through the long summer sunshine the Cottage is stirred
By passers, who brokenly fling them a word:
Such tidings of slaughter! "The enemy cowers;"—
"He breaks!"—"He is flying!"—"Manassas is ours!"

'Tis evening: and Archie, alone on the grass,
Sits watching the fire-flies gleam as they pass,
When sudden he rushes, too eager to wait,—
"Mamma! there's an ambulance stops at the gate!"

Suspense then is past: he is borne from the field,—
"God help me!... God grant it be *not* on his shield!"
And Alice, her passionate soul in her eyes,
And hope and fear winging each quicken'd step, flies,—
Embraces, with frantical wildness, the form
Of her husband, and finds... it is living, and warm!

III.

Ye, who by the couches of languishing ones,
Have watched through the rising and setting of suns,—
Who, silent, behind the close curtain, withdrawn,
Scarce know that the current of being sweeps on,—
To whom outer life is unreal, untrue,
A world with whose moils ye have nothing to do;
Who feel that the day, with its multiform rounds,
Is full of discordant, impertinent sounds,—
Who speak in low whispers, and stealthily tread,
As if a faint footfall were something to dread,—
Who find all existence,—its gladness, its gloom,—
Enclosed by the walls of that limited room,—
Ye only can measure the sleepless unrest
That lies like a night-mare on Alice's breast.

Days come and days go, and she watches the strife
So evenly balanced, 'twixt death and 'twixt life;
Thanks God he still breathes, as each evening takes wing,
And dares not to think what the morrow may bring.

In the lone, ghostly midnight, he raves as he lies,
With death's ashen pallidness dimming his eyes:
He shouts the sharp war-cry,—he rallies his men,—
He is on the red field of Manassas again.

"Now, courage, my comrades! Keep steady! lie low!
Wait, like the couch'd lion, to spring on your foe:
Ye'll face without flinching the cannons' grim mouth,
For ye're 'Knights of the Horse-Shoe'—ye're Sons of the
South!
There's Jackson!—how brave he rides! coursing at will,
Midst the prostrated lines on the crest of the hill;
God keep him! for what will we do if he falls?
Be ready, good fellows!—be cool when he calls
To the charge: Oh! we'll beat them,—we'll turn them,—and
then
We'll ride them down madly!—On! Onward! my men!"

The feverish frenzy o'erwearies him soon,
And back on his pillows he sinks in a swoon.

And sometimes, when Alice is wetting his lip,
He turns from the draught, and refuses to sip:
—"'Tis sweet, pretty angel!—but yonder there lies
A famishing comrade, with death in his eyes:
His need is far greater, ... Sir Philip, I think,—
Or was it Sir Philip?... go, go!—let him drink!"

And oft, with a sort of bewildered amaze,
On her face he would fasten the wistfullest gaze:
—"You are kind, but a hospital nurse cannot be
Like Alice,—my tenderest Alice,—to me.
Oh! I know there's at Beechenbrook, many a tear,
As she asks all the day,—'Will he never be here?'"

But Nature, kind healer! brings sovereignest balm,
And strokes the wild pulses with coolness and calm;

The conflict so equal, so stubborn, is past,
And life gains the hardly-won battle at last.
How sweet through the long convalescence to lie,
And from the low window, gaze out at the sky,
And float, as the zephyrs so tranquilly do,
Aloft in the depths of ineffable blue:—
In painless, delicious half consciousness brood,—
No duties to cumber, no claims to intrude,—
Receptive as childhood, from trouble as free,
And feel it is bliss enough simply, to be!

For Alice,—what pencil can picture her joy,—
So perfect, so thankful, so free from annoy,
As her lips press the lotus-bound chalice, and drain
That exquisite blessedness born out of pain!
Oh! not in her maidenhood, blushing and sweet,
When Douglass first poured out his love at her feet;
And not when a shrinking and beautiful bride,
With worshipping fondness she clung to his side;
And not in those holiest moments of life,
When first she was held to his heart, as his wife;
And never in motherhood's earliest bliss,
Had she tasted a happiness rounded like this!

And Douglass, safe sheltered from war's rude alarms,
Finds Eden's lost precincts again in her arms:
He hears afar off, in the distance, the roar
And the lash of the billows that break on the shore
Of his isle of enchantment,—his haven of rest,—
And rapturous languor steals over his breast.

He bathes in the sunlight of Alice's smiles;
He wraps himself round with love's magical wiles:
His sweet iterations pall not on her ear,—
"*I love you—I love you!*"—she never can hear
That cadence too often; its musical roll
Wakes ever an echoed reply in her soul.

—Do visions of trial, of warning, of woe,
Loom dark in the future of doubt? Do they know
They are hiving, of honied remembrance, a store
To live on, when summer and sunshine are o'er?
Do they feel that their island of beauty at last
Must be rent by the tempest,—be swept by the blast?
Do they dream that afar, on the wild, wintry main,
Their love-freighted bark must be driven again?

—Bless God for the wisdom that curtains so tight
To-morrow's enjoyments or griefs from our sight!
Bless God for the ignorance, darkness and doubt,
That girdle so kindly our future about!

The crutches are brought, and the invalid's strength
Is able to measure the lawn's gravel'd length;
And under the beeches, once more he reclines,
And hears the wind plaintively moan through the pines;
His children around him, with frolic and play,
Cheat autumn's mild listlessness out of the day;
And Alice, the sunshine all flecking her book,
Reads low to the chime of the murmuring brook.

But the world's rushing tide washes up to his feet,
And leaps the soft barriers that bound his retreat;
The tumult of camps surges out on the breeze,
And ever seems mocking his Capuan ease.
He dare not be happy, or tranquil, or blest,
While his soil by the feet of invaders is prest:
What brooks it though still he be pale as a ghost?
—If he languish or fail, let him fail at his post.

The gums by the brook-side are crimson and brown;
The leaves of the ash flicker goldenly down;
The roses that trellis the porches, have lost
Their brightness and bloom at the touch of the frost;
The ozier-twined seat by the beeches, no more
Looks tempting, and cheerful, and sweet, as of yore;
The water glides darkly and mournfully on,
As Alice sits watching it:—Douglass has gone!

IV.

"I am weary and worn,—I am hungry and chill,
And cuttingly strikes the keen blast o'er the hill;
All day I have ridden through snow and through sleet,
With nothing,—not even a cracker to eat;
But now, as I rest by the bivouac fire,
Whose blaze leaps up merrily, higher and higher,
Impatient as Roland, who neighs to be fed,—
For Caleb to bring me my bacon and bread,—
I'll warm my cold heart, that is aching and lone,
By thinking of you, love,—my Alice,—my own!

"I turn a deaf ear to the scream of the wind,
I leave the rude camp and the forest behind;
And Beechenbrook, wrapped in its raiment of white,
Is tauntingly filling my vision to-night.
I catch my sweet little ones' innocent mirth,
I watch your dear face, as you sit at the hearth;
And I know, by the tender expression I see,
I know that my darling is musing of me.
Does her thought dim the blaze?—Does it shed through the
room
A chilly, unseen, and yet palpable gloom?
Ah! then we are equal! *You* share all my pain,
And *I* halve your blessedness with you again!

"Don't think that my hardships are bitter to bear;
Don't think I repine at the soldier's rough fare;
If ever a thought so unworthy steals on,
I look upon Ashby,—and lo! it is gone!
Such chivalry, fortitude, spirit and tone,
Make brighter, and stronger, and prouder, my own.
Oh! Beverly, boy!—on his white steed, I ween,
A princelier presence has never been seen;
And as yonder he lies, from the groups all apart,
I bow to him loyally,—bow with my heart.

"What brave, buoyant letters you write, sweet!—they ring
Through my soul like the blast of a trumpet, and bring
Such a flame to my eye, such a flush to my cheek,—
That often my hand will unconsciously seek
The hilt of my sword as I read,—and I feel
As the warrior does, when he flashes the steel
In fiery circles, and shouts in his might,
For the heroes behind him, to follow its light!
True wife of a soldier!—If doubt or dismay
Had ever, within me, one instant held sway,
Your words wield a spell that would bid them be gone,
Like bodiless ghosts at the touch of the dawn.

"Could the veriest craven that cowers and quails
Before the vast horde that insults and assails
Our land and our liberties,—could he to-night,
Sit here on the ice-girdled log where I write,
And look on the hopeful, bright brows of the men,
Who have toiled all the day over mountain, through glen,—
Half-clothed and unfed,—would he doubt?—would he dare,
In the face of such proof, yield again to despair?

"The hum of their voices comes laden with cheer,
As the wind wafts a musical swell to my ear,—
Wild, clarion catches,—now flute-like and low;
—Would you like me to give you their Song of the Snow?

Halt!—the march is over!
    Day is almost done;
Loose the cumbrous knapsack,
    Drop the heavy gun:

Chilled and wet and weary,
    Wander to and fro,
Seeking wood to kindle
    Fires amidst the snow.

Round the bright blaze gather,
    Heed not sleet nor cold,–
Ye are Spartan soldiers,
    Stout and brave and bold:

Never Xerxian army
    Yet subdued a foe,
Who but asked a blanket
    On a bed of snow.

Shivering midst the darkness
    Christian men are found,
There devoutly kneeling
    On the frozen ground,–

Pleading for their country,
    In its hour of woe,–
For its soldiers marching
    Shoeless through the snow.

Lost in heavy slumbers,
    Free from toil and strife;
Dreaming of their dear ones,–
    Home, and child, and wife;

Tentless they are lying,
    While the fires burn low,–
Lying in their blankets,
    Midst December's snow!

Come, Sophy, my blossom! I've something to say
Will chase for a moment your gambols away:
To-day as we climbed the steep mountain-path o'er,
I noticed a bare-footed lad in my corps;
"How comes it,"–I asked,–"you look careful and bold,
How comes it you're marching, unshod, through the cold?"

"Ah, sir! I'm a poor, lonely orphan, you see;
No mother, no friends that are caring for me;

If I'm wounded, or captured, or killed, in the war,
'Twill matter to nobody, Colonel Dunbar."

Now, Sophy!—your needles, dear!—Knit him some socks,
And send the poor fellow a pair in my box;
Then he'll know,—and his heart with the thought will be
filled,—
There is *one* little maiden will care if he's killed.

The fire burns dimly, and scattered around,
The men lie asleep on the snow-covered ground;
But ere in my blanket I wrap me to rest,
I hold you, my darling, close,—close, to my breast:
God love you! God grant you His comforting light!
I kiss you a thousand times over!—Good night!

V.

"To-morrow is Christmas!"—and clapping his hands,
Little Archie in joyful expectancy stands,
And watches the shadows, now short and now tall,
That momently dance up and down on the wall.

Drawn curtains of crimson shut out the cold night,
And the parlor is pleasant with odours and light;
The soft lamp suspended, its mellowness throws
O'er cluster'd geranium, jasmine and rose;
The sleeping canary hangs caged midst the blooms,
A Sybarite slumberer steeped in perfumes;
For Alice still clings to her birds and her flowers,
Sweet tokens of kindlier, happier hours.

"To-morrow is Christmas!—but Beverly,—say,
Will it do to be glad when Papa is away?"

And the face that is tricksy and blythe as can be,
Tries vainly to temper its shadowless glee.

"For *you*, pet, I'm sure it is right to be glad;
'Tis a pitiful thing to see little ones sad;
But for Sophy and me, who are older, you know,—
We dare not be glad when we look at the snow!
I shrink from this comfort, this light and this heat,
This plenty to wear, and this plenty to eat,
When the soldiers who fight for us,—die for us,—lie,
With nothing around and above, but the sky;
When their clothes are so light, and the rations they deal,
Are only a morsel of bacon and meal:
And how can I fold my thick blankets around,
When I know that my father's asleep on the ground?
I'm ashamed to be happy, or merry, or free,
As if war and its trials were nothing to me:
Oh! I never can know any frolic or fun,—
Any real, mad romps,—till the battles are done!"
And the face of the boy, so heroic and fair,
Is touched with the singular shadow of care.

Sophy ceases her warbling, subdues her soft mirth,
And draws her low ottoman up to the hearth:

"But, brother, what good would it do to refuse
The comforts and blessings God gives us, or use
Them quite with indifference, as much as to say,
We care not how soon they are taken away!
I am sure I would give my last blanket, and spread
My pretty, blue cloak, at night, over my bed,—
(Mamma, you know, covers herself with her shawl,
Since we've sent all our blankets,)—but, then, it's too small!
Would Papa be less hungry or cold, do you think,
If *we* had too little to eat or to drink?
So I mean to be busy,—I mean to be glad;
Mamma says there's time enough yet to be sad;
I'll work for the soldiers,—I'll pray, and I'll plan,
And just be as happy as ever I can;
I've made the grey shirt, and I've finished the socks:—
So come, let us help,—they are packing the box."

How grateful the task is to Alice! her cares
Are quite put aside, and her countenance wears

A look of enjoyment as eager, as bright,
As Santa Claus brings little dreamers to-night;
For Douglass away in his camp, is to share
The daintiest cates that her larder can spare.

The turkey, well seasoned, and tenderly browned,
Is flanked by the spiciest *a la mode* "round;"
The great "priestly ham," in its juiciest pride,
Is there,—with the tenderest surloin beside;
Neat bottles, suggestive of ketchups and wines,
And condiments racy, of various kinds;
And firm rolls of butter as yellow as gold,
And patties and biscuit most rare to behold,
And sauces that richest of odors betray,—
Are marshalled in most appetizing array.
Then Beverly brings of his nuts a full store,
And Archie has apples, a dozen or more;
While Sophy, with gratified housewifery, makes
Her present of spicy "Confederate cakes."

And then in a snug little corner, there lies
A pacquet will brighten the orphan boy's eyes;
For Beverly claims it a pleasure to use
His last cherish'd hoardings in buying him shoes.

Sophy's socks too are there; and she catches afar—
"There's *somebody* cares for me, Colonel Dunbar!"

What subtlest of essences, sovereign to cheer—
What countless, uncatalogu'd tokens are here!
What lavender'd memories, tenderly green,
Lie hidden, these grosser of viands between!
What food for the heart-life,—unreckon'd, untold—
What manna enclosed in its chalice of gold!
What caskets of sweets that Love only unlocks,—
What mysteries Douglass will find in the box!

VI.

The lull of the Winter is over; and Spring
Comes back, as delicious and buoyant a thing,
As airy, and fairy, and lightsome, and bland,
As if not a sorrow was dark'ning the land;—
So little has Nature of passion or part
In the woes and the throes of humanity's heart.

The wild tide of battle runs red,—dashes high,
And blots out the splendour of earth and of sky;
The blue air is heavy, and sulph'rous, and dun,
And the breeze on its wings bears the boom of the gun.
In faster and fiercer and deadlier shocks,
The thunderous billows are hurled on the rocks;
And our Valley becomes, amid Spring's softest breath,
The valley, alas! of the shadow of death.

The crash of the onset,—the plunge and the roll,
Reach down to the depth of each patriot's soul;
It quivers—for since it is human, it must;
But never a tremor of doubt or distrust,
Once blanches the cheek, or is wrung from the mouth,
Or lurks in the eye of the sons of the South.

What need for dismay? Let the live surges roar,
And leap in their fury, our fastnesses o'er,
And threaten our beautiful Valley to fill
With rapine and ruin more terrible still:
What fear we?—See Jackson! his sword in his hand,
Like the stern rocks around him, immovable stand,—
The wisdom, the skill and the strength that he boasts,
Sought ever from him who is Leader of Hosts:
—He speaks in the name of his God:—lo! the tide,—
The red sea of battle, is seen to divide;
The pathway of victory cleaves the dark flood;—
And the foe is o'erwhelmed in a deluge of blood!

The spirit of Alice no longer is bowed
By the troubles, and tumults, and terrors, that crowd
So closely around her:—the willow's lithe form
Bends meekly to meet the wild rush of the storm.

Yet pale as Cassandra, unconscious of joy,
With visions of Greeks at the gates of her Troy,
All day she has waited and watched on the lawn,
Till the purple and gold of the sunset are gone;
For the battle draws near her:—few leagues intervene
Her home and that Valley of slaughter, between.

The tidings and rumors come thick and come fast,
As riders fly hotly and breathlessly past;
They tell of the onslaught,—the headlong attack
Of the foe with a quadruple force at his back:
They boast how they hurl themselves,—shiver and fall
Before their stout rampart, the valiant "Stonewall."

At length, with the gradual fading of day,—
The tokens of battle are floated away:

The booming no longer makes sullen the air,
And the silence of night seems as holy as prayer.

Gray shadows still linger the beeches among,
And scarce has the earliest matin been sung,
Ere Alice with Beverly pale at her side,
Yet firm as his mother, is ready to ride.

With sympathy, womanly, tender, divine,—
With lint and with bandage, with bread and with wine,—
She hastes to the battle-field, eager to bear
Relief to the wounded and perishing there:
To breathe, like an angel of mercy, the breath
Of peace over brows that are fainting in death.

She dares not to stir with a question, *her* woe,
One word,—and the bitter-brimm'd heart would o'erflow:
But speechless, and moveless, and stony of eye,
Scarce conscious of aught in the earth or the sky,
In a swoon of the heart, all her senses have reeled,—
But she prays for endurance,—for here is the field.

The flight and pursuit, so harassing, so hot,
Have drifted all combatants far from the spot:
And through the sparse woodlands, and over the plain,
Lie gorily scattered, the wounded and slain.
Oh! the sickness,—the shudder,—the quailing of fear,
As it leaps to her lips,—"What if Douglass be here!"

Yet she frames not a question; her spirit can bear
Oh! anything,—all things, but hopeless despair:
Does her darling lie stretched on the slope of yon hill?
Let her doubt—let her hug the suspense, if she will!

She watches each ambulance-burden with dread;
She loots in the faces of dying and dead:
And hour after hour, with steady control,
She bends to her task all the strength of her soul;
She comforts the wounded with pity's sweet care,
And the spirit that's passing, she speeds with her prayer.

She starts as she hears, from her stout-hearted boy,
A wild exclamation, half doubt and half joy:—

"Oh! Surgeon!—some brandy! he's fainting!—Ah! now
The colour comes back to his cheek and his brow:—
He breathes again—speaks again—listen!—you are
'An orderly'—is it?—'of Colonel Dunbar?'
'He fought like a lion!' (I knew it!) and passed
Untouched through the battle, 'unhurt to the last?'
—My father is safe,—mother!—safe!—what a joy!
And here is Macpherson,—our barefooted boy!"

Poor Alice!—her grief has been tearless and dumb,
But the pressure once lifted, her senses succumb:
Too quick the revulsion,—too glad the surprise,—
The mists of unconsciousness curtain her eyes:
'Tis only a moment they suffer eclipse,
And words of thanksgiving soon thrill on her lips.

To Beechenbrook's quiet, with tenderest care,
They hasten the wounded, wan soldier to bear;
And never hung mother more patiently o'er
The couch of the child, her own bosom that bore,
Than Alice above the lone orphan, who lay
Submissively breathing his spirit away.

He knows that existence is ebbing; his brain
Is lucid and calm, in the pauses of pain;
But his round boyish cheek with no weeping is wet,
And his smile is not touched with a shade of regret.

No murmur is uttered—no lingering sigh
Escapes him;—so young,—yet so willing to die!
His garment of flesh he has worn undefiled,
His faith is the beautiful faith of a child:
He knows that the Crucified hung on the tree,
That the pathway to bliss might be open and free:
He believes that the cup has been drained,—he can find
Not a drop of the wrath that had filled it,—behind.
If ever a doubt or misgiving assails,
His finger he puts on the print of the nails;
If sometimes there springs an emotion of fear,
He lays his cold hand on the mark of the spear!
He thinks of his darling, dead mother;—the light
Of the Heavenly City falls full on his sight:
And under the rows of the palms, by the brim
Of the river—he knows she is waiting for him.

But the present comes back;—and on Alice's ear,
Fall whispers like these, as she pauses to hear:

"Only a private;—and who will care
    When I may pass away,—
Or how, or why I perish, or where
    I mix with the common clay?
They will fill my empty place again,
    With another as bold and brave;
And they'll blot me out, ere the Autumn rain
    Has freshened my nameless grave.

Only a private:—it matters not,
    That I did my duty well;
That all through a score of battles I fought,
    And then, like a soldier, fell:
The country I died for,—never will heed
    My unrequited claim;
And history cannot record the deed,
    For she never has heard my name.

Only a private;—and yet I know,
    When I heard the rallying call,
I was one of the very first to go,
    And ... I'm one of the many who fall:
But, as here I lie, it is sweet to feel,
    That my honor's without a stain;—
That I only fought for my Country's weal,
    And not for glory or gain.

Only a private;—yet He who reads
    Through the guises of the heart,
Looks not at the splendour of the deeds,
    But the way we do our part;
And when He shall take us by the hand,
    And our small service own,
There'll a glorious band of privates stand
    As victors around the throne!"

The breath of the morning is heavy and chill,
    And gloomily lower the mists on the hill:
The winds through the beeches are shivering low,
    With a plaintive and sad *miserere* of woe:
A quiet is over the Cottage,—a dread
    Clouds the children's sweet faces,—Macpherson is dead!

VII.

'Tis Autumn,—and Nature the forest has hung
With arras more gorgeous than ever was flung
From Gobelin looms,—all so varied, so rare,
As never the princeliest palaces were.
Soft curtains of haze the far mountains enfold,
Whose warp is of purple, whose woof is of gold,
And the sky bends as peacefully, purely above,
As if earth breathed an atmosphere only of love.

But thick as white asters in Autumn, are found
The tents all bestrewing the carpeted ground;
The din of a camp, with its stir and its strife,
Its motley and strange, multitudinous life,
Floats upward along the brown slopes, till it fills
The echoing hollows afar in the hills.

'Tis the twilight of Sabbath,—and sweet through the air,
Swells the blast of the bugle, that summons to prayer:
The signal is answered, and soon in the glen
Sits Colonel Dunbar in the midst of his men.

The Chaplain advances with reverent face,
Where lies a felled oak, he has chosen his place;
On the stump of an ash-tree the Bible he lays,
And they bow on the grass, as he solemnly prays.

Underneath thine open sky,
    Father, as we bend the knee,
May we feel thy presence nigh,
    —Nothing 'twixt our souls and thee!

We are weary,—cares and woes
    Lay their weight on every breast,
And each heart before thee knows,
    That it sighs for inward rest.

Thou canst lift this weight away,
    Thou canst bid these sighings cease;
Thou canst walk these waves and say
    To their restless tossings—"Peace!"

We are tempted;—snares abound,—
    Sin its treacherous meshes weaves;
And temptations strew us round,
    Thicker than the Autumn leaves.

Midst these perils, mark our path,
    Thou who art 'the life, the way;'
Rend each fatal wile that hath
    Power to lead our souls astray.

Prince of Peace! we follow Thee!
    Plant thy banner in our sight;
Let thy shadowy legions be
    Guards around our tents to-night."

Through the aisles of the forest, far-stretching and dim
As a cloister'd Cathedral, the notes of a hymn
Float tenderly upward,—now soft and now clear,
As if twilight had silenced its breathing to hear;
Now swelling, a lofty, triumphant refrain,—
Now sobbing itself into sadness again.

The Bible is opened, and stillness profound
Broods over the listeners scattered around;
And warning, and comfort, and blessing, and balm,
Distil from the beautiful words of the Psalm.
Then simply and earnestly pleading,—his face
Lit up with persuasive and eloquent grace,
The Chaplain pours forth, from the warmth of his heart,
His words of entreaty and truth, ere they part.

"I see before me valiant men,
    With courage high and true,
Who fight as only heroes fight,
    And die, as heroes do.

Your serried ranks have never quailed
    Before the battle-shock,
Whose maddest fury beats and breaks
    Like foam against the rock.

Ye've borne the deadly brunt of war,
    Through storm, and cold, and heat,
Yet never have ye turned your backs
    Nor fled before defeat.

Behind you lie your cheerful homes,
    And all of sweet or fair,—
The only remnants earth has left
    Of Eden-life, are there.

Ye know that many a once bright cheek
    Consuming care, makes wan;
Ye know the old, dear happiness
    That blest your hearths,—is gone.

Ye see your comrades smitten down,—
    The young, the good, the brave,—
Ye feel, the turf ye tread to-day,
    May be to-morrow's grave.

Yet not a murmur meets the ear,
    Nor discontent has sway,
And not a sullen brow is seen,
    Through all the camp to-day.

No Greek, in Greece's palmiest days,
    His javelin ever threw,
Impelled by more heroic zeal,
    Or nobler aim than you.

No mailed warrior ever bore
    Aloft his shining lance,
More proudly through the tales that fire
    The page of old romance.

Oh! soldiers!—well ye bear your part;
    The world awards its praise:
Be sure,—this grandest tourney o'er,—
    'Twill crown you with its bays!

But there's sublimer work than even
    To free your native sod;
—Ye may be loyal to your land,
    Yet traitors to your God!

No Moslem heaven for him who falls,
    A bribed requital doles;
And while ye save your country,—ye,
    Alas! may lose your souls!

No glorious deeds can urge their claim,—
    No merits, entrance win,—
The pierced hand of Christ alone,
    Must freely let you in.

Oh! sirs!—there lurks a fiercer foe,
    Than this that treads your soil,
Who springs from unseen ambuscades,
    To drag you as his spoil.

He drugs the heedless conscience, till,
    No wary watch it keeps,
And parleys with the treacherous heart,
    While fast the warder sleeps.

He captive leads the wavering will
    With specious words, and fair,
And enters the beleaguered soul,
    And rules, a conqueror there.

Will ye who fling defiance forth,
    Against a temporal foe,
And rather die, than stoop to wear
    The chains that gall you so,—

Will ye succumb beneath a power,
    That grasps at full control,
And binds its helpless victims down
    In servitude of soul?

Nay,—act like brave men, as ye are,—
    Nor let the despot, sin,
Wrest those immortal rights away,
    Which Christ has died to win.

For Heaven—best home—true fatherland,
    Bear toil, reproach and loss,
Your highest honor,—holiest name,—
    The soldiers of the Cross!

VIII.

"My Douglass! my darling!—there once was a time,
When we to each other confessed the sublime
And perfect sufficiency love could bestow,
On the hearts that have learned its completeness to know;
We felt that we too had a well-spring of joy,
That earthly convulsions could never destroy,—
A mossy, sealed fountain, so cool and so bright,
It could solace the soul, let it thirst as it might.

"'Tis easy, while happiness strews in our path,
The richest and costliest blessings it hath,
'Tis easy to say that no sorrow, no pain,
Could utterly beggar our spirits again;
'Tis easy to sit in the sunshine, and speak
Of the darkness and storm, with a smile on the cheek!

"As hungry and cold, and with weariness spent,
You droop in your saddle, or crouch in your tent;
Can you feel that the love so entire, so true,
The love that we dreamed of,—is all things to you?
That come what there may,—desolation or loss,
The prick of the thorn, or the weight of the cross—
You can bear it,—nor feel you are wholly bereft,
While the bosom that beats for you only, is left?
While the birdlings are spared that have made it so blest,
Can you look, undismayed, on the wreck of the nest?

"There's a love that is tenderer, sweeter than this—
That is fuller of comfort, and blessing, and bliss;
That never can fail us, whatever befall—
Unchanging, unwearied, undying, through all:
We have need of the support—the staff and the rod;—
Beloved! we'll lean on the bosom of God!

"You guess what I fain would keep hidden:—you know,
Ere now, that the trail of the insolent foe
Leaves ruin behind it, disastrous and dire,
And burns through our Valley, a pathway of fire.
—Our beautiful home,—as I write it, I weep,
Our beautiful home is a smouldering heap!
And blackened, and blasted, and grim, and forlorn,
Its chimneys stand stark in the mists of the morn!

"I stood in my womanly helplessness, weak—
Though I felt a brave color was kindling my cheek—
And I plead by the sacredest things of their lives—
By the love that they bore to their children,—their wives,
By the homes left behind them, whose joys they had shared,
By the God that should judge them,—that mine should be
spared.

"As well might I plead with the whirlwind to stay
As it crashingly cuts through the forest its way!
I know that my eye flashed a passionate ire,
As they scornfully flung me their answer of—fire!

"Why harrow your heart with the grief and the pain?
Why paint you the picture that's scorching my brain?
Why speak of the night when I stood on the lawn,
And watched the last flame die away in the dawn?
'Tis over,—that vision of terror,—of woe!
Its horrors I would not recall;—let them go!
I am calm when I think what I suffered them for;
I grudge not the quota *I* pay to the war!

"But, Douglass!—deep down in the core of my heart,
There's a throbbing, an aching, that will not depart;
For memory mourns, with a wail of despair,
The loss of her treasures,—the subtle, the rare,
Precious things over which she delighted to pore,
Which nothing,—ah! nothing, can ever restore!

"The rose-covered porch, where I sat as your bride—
The hearth, where at twilight I leaned at your side—
The low-cushioned window-seat, where I would lie,
With my head on your knee, and look out on the sky:—
The chamber all holy with love and with prayer,
The motherhood memories clustering there—
The vines that *your* hand has delighted to train,
The trees that *you* planted;—Oh! never again
Can love build us up such a bower of bliss;
Oh! never can home be as hallow'd as this!

"Thank God! there's a dwelling not builded with hands,
Whose pearly foundation, immovable stands;
There struggles, alarms, and disquietudes cease,
And the blissfulest balm of the spirit is—peace!
Small trial 'twill seem when our perils are past,
And we enter the house of our Father at last,—
Light trouble, that here, in the night of our stay,
The blast swept our wilderness lodging away!

"The children—dear hearts!—it is touching to see
My Beverly's beautiful kindness to me;
So buoyant his mein—so heroic—resigned—
The boy has the soul of his father, I find!
Not a childish complaint or regret have I heard,—
Not even from Archie, a petulant word:
Once only—a tear moistened Sophy's bright cheek:
'*Papa has no home now!*'—'twas all she could speak.

"A stranger I wander midst strangers; and yet
I never,—no, not for a moment forget
That my heart has a home,—just as real, as true,
And as warm as if Beechenbrook sheltered me too.
God grant that this refuge from sorrow and pain—
This blessedest haven of peace, may remain!
And, then, though disaster, still sharper, befall,
I think I can patiently bear with it all:
For the rarest, most exquisite bliss of my life
Is wrapped in a word, Douglass ... I am your wife!"

IX.

When fierce and fast-thronging calamities rush
Resistless as destiny o'er us, and crush
The life from the quivering heart till we feel
Like the victim whose body is broke on the wheel—
When we think we have touched the far limit at last,
—One throe, and the point of endurance is passed—
When we shivering hang on the verge of despair—
There still is capacity left us to bear.

The storm of the winter, the smile of the Spring,
No respite, no pause, and no hopefulness bring;
The demon of carnage still breathes his hot breath,
And fiercely goes forward the harvest of death.

Days painfully drag their slow burden along;
And the pulse that is beating so steady and strong,
Stands still, as there comes, from the echoing shore
Of the winding and clear Rappahannock, the roar
Of conflict so fell, that the silvery flood
Runs purple and rapid and ghastly with blood.

—Grand army of martyrs!—though victory waves
Them onward, her march must be over *their* graves:
They feel it—they know it,—yet steadier each
Close phalanx moves into the desperate breach:
Their step does not falter—their faith does not yield,—
For yonder, supreme o'er the fiercely-fought field,
Erect in his leonine grandeur, they see
The proud and magnificent calmness of Lee!

'Tis morn—but the night has brought Alice no rest:
The roof seems to press like a weight on her breast;
And she wanders forth, wearily lifting her eye,
To seek for relief 'neath the calm of the sky.

The air of the forest is spicy and sweet,
And dreamily babbles a brook at her feet;
Her children are 'round her, and sunshine and flowers,
Try vainly to banish the gloom of the hours.
With a volume she fain her wild thoughts would assuage,
But her vision can trace not a line on the page,
And the poet's dear strains, once so soft to her ear,
Have lost all their mystical power to cheer.

The evening approaches—the pressure—the woe
Grows drearer and heavier,—yet she must go,
And stifle between the dead walls, as she may,
The heart that scarce breathed in the free, open day.

She reaches the dwelling that serves as her home;
A horseman awaits at the entrance;—the foam
Is flecking the sides of his fast-ridden steed,
Who pants, over-worn with exhaustion and speed;
And Alice for support to Beverly clings,
As the soldier delivers the letter he brings.

Her ashy lips move, but the words do not come,
And she stands in her whiteness, bewildered and dumb:
She turns to the letter with hopeless appeal,
But her fingers are helpless to loosen the seal:
She lifts her dim eyes with a look of despair,—
Her hands for a moment are folded in prayer;
The strength she has sought is vouchsafed in her need:
—"I think I can bear it now, Beverly .., read."

The boy, with the resolute nerve of a man,
And a voice which he holds as serene as he can,
Takes quietly from her the letter, and reads:—

"Dear Madam,—My heart in its sympathy bleeds
For the pain that my tidings must bear you: may God
Most tenderly comfort you, under His rod!

"This morning, at daybreak, a terrible charge
Was made on the enemy's centre: such large
And fresh reinforcements were held at his back,
He stoutly and stubbornly met the attack.

"Our cavalry bore themselves splendidly:—far
In front of his line galloped Colonel Dunbar;
Erect in his stirrups,—his sword flashing high,
And the look of a conqueror kindling his eye,
His silvery voice rang aloft through the roar
Of the musketry poured from the opposite shore:
—'Remember the Valley!—remember your wives!
And on to your duty, boys!—on—with your lives!'

"He turned, and he paused, as he uttered the call—
Then reeled in his seat, and fell,—pierced by a ball.

"He lives and he breathes yet:—the surgeons declare,
That the balance is trembling 'twixt hope and despair.
In his blanket he lies, on the hospital floor,—
So calm, you might deem all his agony o'er;
And here, as I write, on his face I can see
An expression whose radiance is startling to me.
His faith is sublime:—he relinquishes life,
And craves but one blessing,—*to look on his wife!*"

The Chaplain's recital is ended:—no word
From Alice's white, breathless lips has been heard;
Till, rousing herself from her passionless woe,
She simply and quietly says—"I will go."

There are moments of anguish so deadly, so deep—
That numbness seems over the senses to creep,
With interposition, whose timely relief,
Is an anodyne-draught to the madness of grief.
Such mercy is meted to Alice;—her eye
That sees as it saw not, is vacant and dry:
The billows' wild fury sweeps over her soul,
And she bends to the rush with a passive control.

Through the dusk of the night—through the glare of the day,
She urges, unconscious, her desolate way:
One image is ever her vision before,
—That blanketed form on the hospital floor!

Her journey is ended; and yonder she sees
The spot where *he* lies, looming white through the trees:
Her torpor dissolves with a shuddering start,
And a terrible agony clutches her heart.

The Chaplain advances to meet her:—he draws
Her silently onward;—no question—no pause—
Her finger she lays on her lip;—if she spake,
She knows that the spell that upholds her, would break.

She has strength to go forward; they enter the door,—
And there, on the crowded and blood-tainted floor,
Close wrapped in his blanket, lies Douglass:—his brow
Wore never a look so seraphic as now!
She stretches her arms the dear form to enfold,—
God help her! . . . , she shrieks . . . , it is silent and cold!

X.

"Break, my heart, and ease this pain—
Cease to throb, thou tortured brain;
Let me die,—since he is slain,
    —Slain in battle!

Blessed brow, that loved to rest
Its dear whiteness on my breast—
Gory was the grass it prest,
    —Slain in battle!

Oh! that still and stately form—
Never more will it be warm;
Chilled beneath that iron storm,
　　—Slain in battle!

Not a pillow for his head—
Not a hand to smooth his bed—
Not one tender parting said,
　　—Slain in battle!

Straightway from that bloody sod,
Where the trampling horsemen trod—
Lifted to the arms of God;
　　—Slain in battle!

Not my love to come between,
With its interposing screen—
Naught of earth to intervene;
　　—Slain in battle!

Snatched the purple billows o'er,
Through the fiendish rage and roar,
To the far and peaceful shore;
　　—Slain in battle!

Nunc demitte—thus I pray—
What else left for me to say,
Since my life is reft away?
　　—Slain in battle!

Let me die, oh! God!—the dart
Rankles deep within my heart,—
Hope, and joy, and peace, depart;
　　—Slain in battle!"

'Tis thus through her days and her nights of despair,
Her months of bereavement so bitter to bear,
That Alice moans ever. Ah! little they know,
Who look on that brow, still and white as the snow,
Who watch—but in vain—for the sigh or the tear,
That only comes thick when no mortal is near,—
Who whisper—"How gently she bends to the rod!"
Because all her heart-break is kept for her God,—
Ah! little *they* know of the tempests that roll
Their desolate floods through the depths of her soul!

Afar in our sunshiny homes on the shore,
We heed not how wildly the billows may roar;
We smile at our firesides, happy and free,
While the rich-freighted argosy founders at sea!
Though wrapped in the weeds of her widowhood, pale,—
Though life seems all sunless and dim through the veil
That drearily shadows her sorrowful brow,—
Is the cause of her country less dear to her now?

Does the patriot-flame in her heart cease to stir,—
Does she feel that the conflict is over for her?
Because the red war-tide has deluged her o'er,—
Has wreaked its wild wrath, and can harm *her* no more,—
Does she stand, self-absorbed, on the wreck she has braved,
Nor care if her country be lost or be saved?

By her pride in the soil that has given her birth—
By her tenderest memories garnered on earth—
By the legacy blood-bought and precious, which she
Would leave to her children—the right to be free,—
By the altar where once rose the hymn and the prayer;
By the home that lies scarred in its solitude there,—
By the pangs she has suffered,—the ills she has borne,—
By the desolate exile through which she must mourn,—
By the struggles that hallow this fair Southern sod,
By the vows she has breathed in the ear of her God,—

By the blood of the heart that she worshipped,—the life
That enfolded her own; by her love, as his wife;
By his death on the battle-field, gallantly brave,—
By the shadow that ever will wrap her—his grave—
By the faith she reposes, oh! Father! in Thee,
She claims that her glorious South MUST BE FREE!

VIRGINIA

A SONNET

Grandly thou fillest the world's eye to-day,
    My proud Virginia! When the gage was thrown—
    The deadly gage of battle—thou, alone,
Strong in thy self-control, didst stoop to lay
The olive-branch thereon, and calmly pray
    We might have peace, the rather. When the foe
    Turned scornfully upon thee,—bade thee go,
And whistled up his war-hounds, then—the way
    Of duty full before thee,—thou didst spring
    Into the centre of the martial ring—
Thy brave blood boiling, and thy glorious eye,
    Shot with heroic fire, and swear to claim
    Sublimest victory in God's own name,—
Or, wrapped in robes of martyrdom,—to die!

JACKSON

A SONNET

Thank God for such a Hero!—Fearless hold
    His diamond character beneath the sun,
    And brighter scintillations, one by one,
Come flashing from it. Never knight of old
Wore on serener brow, so calm, yet bold,
    Diviner courage: never martyr knew
    Trust more sublime,—nor patriot, zeal more true,—
Nor saint, self-abnegation of a mould
    Touched with profounder beauty. All the rare,
Clear, starry points of light, that gave his soul
    Such lambent lustre, owned but one sole aim,—
    Not for himself, nor yet his country's fame,
These glories shone: he kept the clustered whole
    A jewel for the crown that Christ shall wear!

DIRGE FOR ASHBY

Heard ye that thrilling word—
 Accent of dread—
Flash like a thunderbolt,
 Bowing each head—
Crash through the battle dun,
Over the booming gun—
"Ashby, our bravest one,—
 Ashby is dead!"

Saw ye the veterans—
 Hearts that had known
Never a quail of fear,
 Never a groan—
Sob 'mid the fight they win,
—Tears their stern eyes within,—
"Ashby, our Paladin,
 Ashby is gone!"

Dash,—dash the tear away—
 Crush down the pain!
"Dulce et decus," be
 Fittest refrain!
Why should the dreary pall
Round him be flung at all?
Did not our hero fall
 Gallantly slain?

Catch the last word of cheer
 Dropt from his tongue;
Over the volley's din,
 Loud be it rung—
"Follow me! follow me!"—
Soldier, oh! could there be
Pæan or dirge for thee,
 Loftier sung!

Bold as the Lion-heart,
      Dauntless and brave;
Knightly as knightliest
      Bayard could crave;
Sweet with all Sidney's grace—
Tender as Hampden's face—
Who—who shall fill the space
Void by his grave?

'Tis not *one* broken heart,
      Wild with dismay;
Crazed with her agony,
      Weeps o'er his clay:
Ah! from a thousand eyes
Flow the pure tears that rise;
Widowed Virginia lies
      Stricken to-day!

Yet—though that thrilling word—
      Accent of dread—
Falls like a thunderbolt,
      Bowing each head—
Heroes! be battle done
Bravelier every one,
Nerved by the thought alone—
      Ashby is dead!

STONEWALL JACKSON'S GRAVE[1]

A simple, sodded mound of earth,
　　Without a line above it;
With only daily votive flowers
　　To prove that any love it:
The token flag that silently
　　Each breeze's visit numbers,
Alone keeps martial ward above
　　The hero's dreamless slumbers.

No name?—no record? Ask the world;
　　The world has read his story—
If all its annals can unfold
　　A prouder tale of glory:—
If ever merely human life
　　Hath taught diviner moral,—
If ever round a worthier brow
　　Was twined a purer laurel!

A twelvemonth only, since his sword
　　Went flashing through the battle—
A twelvemonth only, since his ear
　　Heard war's last deadly rattle—
And yet, have countless pilgrim-feet
　　The pilgrim's guerdon paid him,
And weeping women come to see
　　The place where they have laid him.

1　In the month of June the singular spectacle was presented at
　Lexington, Va., of two hostile armies, in turn, reverently visit-
　ing Jackson's grave.

Contending armies bring, in turn,
  Their meed of praise or honor,
And Pallas here has paused to bind
  The cypress wreath upon her:
It seems a holy sepulchre,
  Whose sanctities can waken
Alike the love of friend or foe,—
  Of Christian or of pagan.

They come to own his high emprise,
  Who fled in frantic masses,
Before the glittering bayonet
  That triumphed at Manassas:
Who witnessed Kernstown's fearful odds,
  As on their ranks he thundered,
Defiant as the storied Greek,
  Amid his brave three hundred!

They well recall the tiger spring,
  The wise retreat, the rally,
The tireless march, the fierce pursuit,
  Through many a mountain valley:
Cross Keys unlock new paths to fame,
  And Port Republic's story
Wrests from his ever-vanquish'd foes,
  Strange tributes to his glory.

Cold Harbor rises to their view,—
  The Cedars' gloom is o'er them;
Antietam's rough and rugged heights,
  Stretch mockingly before them:
The lurid flames of Fredericksburg
  Right grimly they remember,
That lit the frozen night's retreat,
  That wintry-wild December!

The largess of their praise is flung
    With bounty, rare and regal;
—Is it because the vulture fears
    No longer the dead eagle?
Nay, rather far accept it thus,—
    An homage true and tender,
As soldier unto soldier's worth,—
    As brave to brave will render,

But who shall weigh the wordless grief
    That leaves in tears its traces,
As round their leader crowd again,
    The bronzed and veteran faces!
The "Old Brigade" he loved so well—
    The mountain men, who bound him
With bays of their own winning, ere
    A tardier fame had crowned him;

The legions who had seen his glance
    Across the carnage flashing,
And thrilled to catch his ringing *"charge"*
    Above the volley crashing;—
Who oft had watched the lifted hand,
    The inward trust betraying,
And felt their courage grow sublime,
    While they beheld him praying!

Good knights and true as ever drew
    Their swords with knightly Roland;
Or died at Sobieski's side,
    For love of martyr'd Poland;
Or knelt with Cromwell's Ironsides;
    Or sang with brave Gustavus;
Or on the plain of Austerlitz,
    Breathed out their dying aves!

Rare fame! rare name!—If chanted praise,
    With all the world to listen,—
If pride that swells a nation's soul,—
    If foemen's tears that glisten,—
If pilgrims' shrining love,—if grief
    Which nought may soothe or sever,—
If these can consecrate,—this spot
    Is sacred ground forever!

WHEN THE WAR IS OVER

A CHRISTMAS LAY

I.

Ah! the happy Christmas times!
    Times we all remember;—
Times that flung a ruddy glow
    O'er the gray December;—
Will they never come again,
    With their song and story?
Never wear a remnant more
    Of their olden glory?
Must the little children miss
    Still the festal token?
Must their realm of young romance
    All be marred and broken?
Must the mother promise on,
    While her smiles dissemble,
And she speaks right quietly,
    Lest her voice should tremble:—

"Darlings! wait till father comes—
    Wait—and we'll discover
Never were such Christmas times,
    When the war is over!"

II.

Underneath the midnight sky,
      Bright with starry beauty,
Sad, the shivering sentinel
      Treads his round of duty:
For his thoughts are far away,
      Far from strife and battle,
As he listens dreamingly,
      To his baby's prattle;—
As he clasps his sobbing wife,
      Wild with sudden gladness,
Kisses all her tears away—
      Chides her looks of sadness—
Talks of Christmas nights to come,—
      And his step grows lighter,
Whispering, while his stiffening hand
      Grasps his musket tighter:—

"Patience, love!—keep heart! keep hope!
      To your weary rover,
What a home our home will be,
      When the war is over!"

III.

By the twilight Christmas fire,
　　All her senses laden
With a weight of tenderness,
　　Sits the musing maiden:
From the parlor's cheerful blaze,
　　Far her visions wander,
To the white tent gleaming bright,
　　On the hill-side yonder.
Buoyant in her brave, young love,
　　Flushed with patriot honour,
No misgiving, no fond fear,
　　Flings its shade upon her.
Though no mortal soul can know
　　Half the love she bears him,
Proudly, for her country's sake,
　　From her heart she spares him.

—God be thanked!—she does not dream,
　　That her gallant lover
Will be in a soldier's grave,
　　When the war is over!

IV.

'Midst the turmoil and the strife
 Of the war-tide's rushing,
Every heart its separate woe
 In its depths is hushing.
Who has time for tears, when blood
 All the land is steeping?
—In our poverty we grudge
 Even the waste of weeping!
But when quiet comes again,
 And the bands, long broken,
Gather round the hearth, and breathe
 Names now seldom spoken—
Then we'll miss the precious links—
 Mourn the empty places—
Read the hopeless "*Nevermore*,"
 In each other's faces!

—Oh! what aching, anguish'd hearts
 O'er lone graves will hover,
With a new, fresh sense of pain,
 When the war is over!

V.

Stern endurance, bitterer still,
    Sharp with self-denial,
Fraught with loftier sacrifice,
    Fuller far of trial—
Strews our flinty path of thorns—
    Marks our bloody story—
Fits us for the victor's palm—
    Weaves our robe of glory!
Shall we faint with God above,
    And His strong arm under—
And the cold world gazing on,
    In a maze of wonder?
No! with more resistless march,
    More resolved endeavor,
Press we onward—struggle still,
    Fight and win forever!

—Holy peace will heal all ills,
    Joy all losses cover,
Raptures rend our Southern skies,
    When the war is over!

VIRGINIA CAPTA

APRIL 9th, 1865

I.

Unconquered captive!—close thine eye,
  And draw the ashen sackcloth o'er,
And in thy speechless woe deplore
  The fate that would not let thee die!

II.

The arm that wore the shield, strip bare;
  The hand that held the martial rein,
And hurled the spear on many a plain—
  Stretch—till they clasp the shackles there!

III.

The foot that once could crush the crown,
  Must drag the fetters, till it bleed
Beneath their weight:—thou dost not need
  It now, to tread the tyrant down.

IV.

Thou thought'st him vanquish'd—boastful trust!
  —His lance, in twain—his sword, a wreck—
But with his heel upon thy neck,
  He holds *thee* prostrate in the dust!

V.

Bend though thou must, beneath his will,
  Let not one abject moan have place;
But with majestic, silent grace,
  Maintain thy regal bearing still.

VI.

Look back through all thy storied past,
    And sit erect in conscious pride:—
No grander heroes ever died—
    No sterner, battled to the last!

VII.

Weep, if thou wilt, with proud, sad mein,
    Thy blasted hopes—thy peace undone,—
Yet brave, live on,—nor seek to shun
    Thy fate, like Egypt's conquer'd Queen.

VIII.

Though forced a captive's place to fill,
    In the triumphal train,—yet there,
Superbly, like Zenobia, wear
    Thy chains,—*Virginia Victrix* still!

www.ingramcontent.com/pod-product-compliance
Lightning Source LLC
Chambersburg PA
CBHW031526040426
42445CB00009B/420